All the
All the Bad

Dad

Jokes

Brian Pearl

How can you tell if an ant is a boy or girl?
They're all girls; otherwise they'd be uncles.

Where did the one-legged waitress work?
Ihop!

Why did the cookie cry?
Because his father was a wafer so long!

Did I tell you the time I fell in love during a backflip?
I was head over heels.

Where do animals go when their tails fall off?
The re-tail store.

What do you call a lost wolf?
A where-wolf.

How does a train eat?
It goes chew chew.

Did you hear about the magician who was driving down the street?
He turned into a driveway!

How do you get rid of an itch?
Start from scratch.

Why can't Elsa have a balloon?
Because she'll let it go, let it go.

How can you tell if a clock is hungry?
It goes back for seconds.

What do you call a baby monkey?
A chimp off the old block.

What did the big chimney say to the little chimney?
"You are way too young to smoke!"

If one is single and two is a couple and three is a crowd, what are four and five?
Nine.

What do you call a fairy that doesn't bathe?
Stinkerbell.

When is it a good time to eat a window?
When it's jammed.

What's the laziest part of the car?
The wheels because they're tired.

What is the coldest country in South America?
Chile.

What kind of shoes do artists wear?
Sketchers.

What pools are safe for diving?
Deep ends.

Did you hear about the lumberjack who died?
The police are calling it an axe-ident.

Why does a milking stool only have three legs?
Because the cow has the udder.

What kind of driver never gets a parking ticket?
A screwdriver.

Did you hear about the sick juggler?
He couldn't stop throwing up.

What's the worst thing about ancient history class?
The teachers tend to Babylon.

What does a house wear?
A dress.

How do you make antifreeze?
Steal her sweater.

Do you want to hear a chimney joke?
The first one's on the house.

How do you make holy water?
You boil the hell out of it.

What kind of jokes do you make in the shower?
Clean ones.

Where do bees go to the bathroom?
The BP Station.

How do you drown a hipster?
In the mainstream.

What did the hospitalized comic say?
"I'm here, all weak!"

How did the skeleton know what would happen next?
He could feel it in his bones.

Why did the man take care of his stepladder?
Because he never knew his real ladder.

A man tells his doctor, "Help me, I'm addicted to Twitter."
The doctor replies, "Sorry, I don't follow you."

How did the hipster burn his mouth?
He drank his Triple, Venti, Half Sweet, Non-Fat, Caramel Macchiato before it was cool.

How does a Jedi sing in the mountains?
He yoda-ls!

What do you call a fish with no eyes?
A fsh.

Why can't you have a nose that's is twelve inches long?
Because then it would be a foot.

What days are the strongest?
Saturday and Sunday. The rest are week days.

How you ever heard of a music group called cellophane?
They mostly wrap.

What do you call David after he loses his ID?
Dav.

Why are skeletons so calm?
Because nothing gets under their skin.

What is the difference between a hippo and a zippo?
One is really heavy and the other is a little lighter.

What was the robot angry?
Someone kept pushing his buttons.

What did the nut say when it was chasing the other nut?
I'm a cashew!

What are elevator jokes so good?
Because they work on so many levels.

What do you call a nose that can see into the future?
Nostril-damus.

What did one strawberry say to the other?
If you weren't so fresh, we wouldn't be in this jam!

What do you call a woman who can't stand up straight?
Eileen.

What do mermaids wash their fins with?
Tide.

What did one llama say to the other before their holiday?
Alpaca my bags.

What do you call a cow that can't produce milk?
An udder failure.

What do you call a restaurant that only serves Russian gangsters?
Red Mobster.

What did the snow cone say when it got its vision back?
Icey!

Did you hear about the guy who didn't want a brain transplant?
He changed his mind.

Why did the woman hit her husband with stringed instruments?
She had history of violins.

Did you hear about the stolen toilet at the precinct?
The police have nothing to go on.

Did you hear about the two silk worms in the race?
They ended in a tie.

Why was the cellphone wearing glasses?
He lost all his contacts.

What do you call the security outside of a Samsung store?
Guardians of the Galaxy.

What's the difference between a good joke and bad joke timing?

Why shouldn't you tell a secret on a farm?
Because the potatoes have eyes and the corn have ears.

What did the librarian say when the books were a mess?
We ought to be ashamed of our shelves!

What does time fly like?
An arrow.

What does fruit fly like?
A banana.

What's the worst part about movie theater candy prices?
They're always rasinet.

What did the beach say as the tide came in?
Long time, no sea.

Did you hear my song about a tortilla?
Actually, it's more of a wrap.

Did you hear about the man who tried to catch fog?
He mist.

Why do hamburgers go to the gym?
To get better buns.

What did the bird say to the cheating parrot?
Toucan play at that game!

What do you do with chemists when they die?
Barium.

What is Santa's favorite pizza?
One that's deep pan, crisp and even.

How does a muppet die?
It Kermits suicide.

What do you call the heavy breathing someone makes while trying to hold a yoga pose?
Yoga pants.

What kind of dogs like car racing?
Lap dogs.

How do hens cheer for their team?
They egg them on.

What was the student's report card wet?
It was below 'C' level.

Did the disappointed smoker get everything he wanted for Christmas?
Clothes, but no cigar.

What do you call an unpredictable, out of control photographer?
A loose Canon.

How do you impress a baker's daughter?
Bring her flours.

Did you hear about the sensitive burglar?
He takes thing personally.

Why did the rock band hire the turkey?
He came with drumsticks.

Where do New York dads go to get new jokes?
Corny Island.

When is a door not a door?
When it's ajar.

Why didn't the bartender serve the wig?
It forgot toupee.

What happens if a frog parks illegally?
He gets toad.

Why did the barber win the race?
He knew a short cut.

What jam can't you eat?
Traffic.

How much did the pirate's new earrings cost him?
A buccaneer.

What do you calla group of killer whales playing instruments?
An orca-stra.

Why did the octopus beat the shark in a fight?
Because it was well armed.

What did the bartender say to the jumper cable?
"I'll serve you, but don't start anything."

Where can you get chicken broth in bulk?
The stock market.

Did you hear about the guy who invented Altoids?
They say he made a mint.

Why did the Clydesdale give the pony a glass of water?
Because he was a little horse.

What is Beethoven's favorite fruit?
A ba-na-NA-NA!

What is the most popular blood type?
Red.

What kind of pictures do turtles take?
Shellfies.

What did the red light say to the green light?
"Don't look, I'm changing!"

What do you call a poor neighborhood in Italy?
A spaghetto.

How do crazy people get through the forest?
They take the psycho-path.

Want to hear a joke about construction?
Sorry, I'm still working on it.

Did you hear about the mother who gave birth in the sky?
The baby was airborne.

Why did the scarecrow win an award?
Because he was outstanding in his field.

What do you call cheese that isn't yours?
Nacho cheese.

Why did the robber take a bath?
Because he wanted to make a clean getaway.

What lights up a soccer stadium?
A soccer match.

How do you find a princess?
You follow foot prince.

What did one toilet say to the other toilet?
You look flushed.

What do you call an old person with really good hearing?
Deaf defying.

Why couldn't the man stop pretending to be butter?
He was on a roll.

How does Darth Vader like his toast?
On the dark side.

Where do you learn how to make ice cream?
Sundae school.

What do you call a factory that makes OK products?
A satis-factory.

What do you call a person who sees a robbery at an Apple store?
Iwitness.

Did you hear about the piece of paper?
It's so tearable.

Where were French fries first made?
Greece.

Why was the math book sad?
It had too many problems.

Why do watermelons have fancy weddings?
Because they cantaloupe.

Did you hear about the two bed bugs that met in the mattress?
They married in the spring.

How do baseball players stay so cool?
They sit next to their fans.

What did the overly excited gardener do when spring finally arrived?
He wet his plants.

How much does a hipster weigh?
An Instagram.

Why does Waldo wear a striped shirt?
Because he doesn't want to be spotted.

What's green and sings?
Elvis Parsley.

What do you get when you cross Speedy Gonzalez with a country singer?
Arriba McEntire.

What is a tree's favorite drink?
Root beer.

Where does bad light go?
Prism.

What music are balloons scared of?
Pop music.

How does a penguin build his house?
Igloos it together.

What do you call a fake noodle?
An impasta.

Why did the coffee file a police report?
It got mugged.

How many apples grow on a Granny
Smith apple tree?
All of them.

If April showers bring May flowers, what
do May flowers bring?
Pilgrims.

Have you heard they don't need the Golden Gate Bridge an longer?
Because it's already long enough.

Why did the cookie go to the hospital?
Because he felt crummy.

What did the policeman say to his shirt?
You're under a vest.

What do you call a man in a life vest floating in the water?
Bob.

What do you call a man lying by your front door?
Matt.

What lies at the bottom of the ocean and twitches?
A nervous wreck.

What did the frog that was always being bossed around say?
"I just do what I'm toad."

What did the pirate say on his 80th birthday?
Aye, matey!

How many optometrists does it take to change a light bulb?
1 or 2? 1 or 2?

Have you seen the new movie about trees in love?
It's pretty sappy.

Why do bears have hairy coats?
Fur protection.

Did you hear about the magic tractor?
It turned into a field.

What do you call a cow with two legs?
Lean beef.

What do you call a cow with no legs?
Ground beef.

Why shouldn't you trust atoms?
They make up everything.

Did you hear about the circus fire?
It was in tents.

What do you call a nose without a body?
Nobody nose.

How do dogs party?
They raise the woof!

Why do cows have bells?
Because their horns don't work.

How does Moses make his coffee?
Hebrews it.

What did the left eye say to the right eye?
**Between you and me something
smells**.

Why do bananas need sunscreen?
Because they peel.

Want to hear my pizza joke?
Never mind it's too cheesy.

What to hear a word I just made up?
Plagiarism.

What unit of measure is used for snakes?
Inches, they don't feet.

Why wasn't the computer hungry?
He just had a byte.

What's a margarita lover's favorite book?
Tequila Mockingbird.

What kind of person wears two watches at once?
Someone with too much time on their hands.

What did the buffalo say when he dropped his son off at school?
"Bison."

Why did the crab never share?
He was shellfish.

Why wasn't the woman happy with the Velcro she bought?
It was a total rip off.

What does an angry pepper do?
Gets jalapeno your face.

What do you call a person in a tree with a briefcase?
A branch manager.

What's brown and sounds like a bell?
Duuuuuuung.

What do you give a sick bird?
Tweetment.

What do you call a snobbish prisoner going down the stairs?
A condescending con descending.

Did I tell you about my new bowling team?
"I can't believe it's not gutter."

What did the Tin Man say when get got run over?
Curses, foil again!

What do Black Friday shoppers and the Thanksgiving turkey have in common?
They know what it's like to be stuffed and then jammed into a small place.

Why did the chicken go to the séance?
To get to the other side.

When were vowels invented?
When U and I were born.

What has four wheels and flies?
A garbage truck.

What's orange and sounds like a parrot?
A carrot.

What do you call a car that everyone can buy?
A-ford.

Why didn't the man like Civil War jokes?
He didn't General Lee find them funny.

Why did the coffee taste like mud?
It was fresh ground yesterday.

What should you do if someone calls you "odd"?
Get even.

Did you hear about he kidnapping at school?
It's all right, he woke up.

Want to hear two short jokes and a long joke.
Joke. Joke. Joooooooooooooooooke.

Why didn't the wrestler get a new haircut?
He had to mullet over.

What do you call Santa's helpers?
Subordinate clauses.

Why does Peter Pan always fly?
He never lands.

What's the best way to carve wood?
Whittle by whittle.

Why did the picture go to jail?
Because he was framed.

What type of music do mummies listen to?
Wrap music.

What did the finger say to the thumb?
I'm in glove with you.

What do you call a snowman with a six-pack?
An abdominal snowman.

What's the difference between roast beef and pea soup?
You can roast beef!

What do you call a crushed angle?
A rectangle.

What do you call leftover aliens?
Extra terrestrials.

Where is an astronaut's favorite place on the keyboard?
The space bar.

Why is basketball such a messy sport?
All the dribbling.

What exam do young witches have to pass?
A spell-ing test.

Why runs but doesn't get anywhere?
A refrigerator.

What do you call a lobster with a Christmas hat?
Santa Claws.

How do you make a tissue dance?
You put a little boogie in it.

What did the miner need glasses?
He had tunnel vision.

Why will Kim Jong-Un never use nuclear weapons?
He's afraid it will cost him his Korea.

What do you give a dog with a fever?
Mustard, it's the best thing for a hot dog.

What did the digital watch say to the grandfather clock?
"Look gramps, no hands!"

What do cats eat for breakfast?
Mice Crispies.

How do you communicate with a fish?
Drop him a line.

What do you call a bear with no teeth?
A gummy bear.

What do you call a religious person that sleepwalks?
A roamin' Catholic.

Where do snowmen keep their money?
Snow banks.

What do you call a musician with problems?
A trebled man.

What do you call a priest that becomes a lawyer?
A father-in-law.

What did the police say when the raided the seafood restaurant?
Don't move a mussel!

What happened when the man lost his job at the mint factory?
He went absolutely menthol.

What did the casket say to the other casket?
Is that you coffin?

Why did the cowboy adopt a miniature dachshund?
Because he wanted to get a long lil' doggie.

Did you hear about the new restaurant they opened on the moon?
The food is great but there's just no atmosphere.

Why do Italians like sharp angles?
Because they're acute.

What's brown and sticky?
A stick.

What's the difference between ignorance and apathy?
I don't know and I don't care.

Where do hamburgers go to dance?
The meat ball.

Why are penguins socially awkward?
Because they can't break the ice.

Why did the poor man sell yeast?
To raise some dough.

Why did the man stand on one leg at the bank?
He was checking his balance.

What do you call a Frenchman who wears beach sandals?
Philippe Phil-loppe.

Why should you never use a dull pencil?
Because it's pointless.

What's the funniest plant in the desert?
The yuk-ka plant.

What do you call someone who's afraid of Santa?
A Claus-trophobic.

Why do the cross-eyed teacher lose her job?
She couldn't control her pupils.

What is the best season for trampoline?
Springtime.

What do you call a laughing motorcycle?
A Yamaha-haha.

What did the bald man say when he
received a comb as a gift?
"Gee, I'll never part with it!"

Who delivers Christmas presents to good
little sharks when they're sleeping?
Santa Jaws.

What do you get when you combine a
Christmas tree with an iPad?
Pineapple.

Why are Comet, Cupid, Donner and
Blitzen always wet?
Because they are rain deer.

Why do moon rocks taste better than
earth rock?
Because they're meteor.

What do you call a waterfowl that looks in your windows?
A Peking duck.

What do you call a bird that is afraid of heights?
A chicken.

Is there an advantage to living in Switzerland?
No, but the flag is a big plus.

What did one snowman say to the other snowman?
"Do you smell carrots?"

What's large gray and doesn't matter?
An irrelephant.

What does a baby computer call his father?
Data.

What do hillbillies drink out of?
Hic-cups.

What time did the man get to Wimbledon?
Tennish.

What kind of bagel can fly?
A plane bagel.

What do you call a zoo with only one dog?
A Shih Tzu.

How many South Americans does it take to change a light bulb?
A Brazilian.

Where does the general keep his armies?
In his sleevies.

Did you hear about the guy who invented the door knocker?
He won the no-bell prize.

Did you hear about the guy who's afraid of elevators?
He's taking steps to avoid them.

What time of day was Adam born?
A little before Eve.

What's the difference between in-laws and outlaws?
Outlaws are wanted.

What often gets overlooked?
Fences.

Why can't the man plant flowers?
He hadn't botany.

What's the leading cause of dry skin?
Towels.

Why is England the wettest country?
Because the queen has reigned there for **years.**

Why did the man put his money in the freezer?
He wanted cold hard cash.

Why are pirates called pirates?
Because they Arrrrrrrrr!

Why did the computer go to the doctor?
It had a virus.

What do you call a magician on the plane?
A flying sorcerer.

What kind of shorts do clouds wear?
Thunderwear.

What happened to the wooden car with wooden wheels and wooden engine?
It wooden't go.

Which month do soldiers hate most?
The month of March.

What happened to the cow that jumped over the barbed wire fence?
Udder destruction.

What did the Buddhist ask the hot dog vendor?
Make me one with everything.

Who wanders if their uniform makes him look bad?
An insecurity guard.

How does the moon cut his hair?
Eclipse it.

Why did the man delay his trip to Moscow?
There is no point Russian into things.

How many ears does Captain Kirk have?
Three - the left ear, the right ear and the final front ear.

Why was the calendar for afraid?
Its days were numbered.

Why was the Energizer Bunny arrested?
Battery.

When the Mystery Machine breaks down, who has to go for help?
Scooby-Doo.

Did you hear about the lumberjack who was fired for cutting down too many trees?
He saw too much.

What did the beaver say to the tree?
It's been nice gnawin' you.

Why is no one friends with Dracula?
Because he's a pain in the neck.

Why can't you hear a pterodactyl go to the bathroom?
Because the 'p' is silent.

Can February March?
No, but April May.

What does a vegetarian zombie eat?
Grains.

What do you call a lonely cheese?
Provolone.

What do you call a nervous javelin thrower?
Shakespeare.

Did you hear about the astronaut who stepped on chewing gum?
He got stuck in orbit.

Did you hear about the calendar thief?
He got 12 months.

What happens if life gives you melons?
You're dyslexic.

Why did C-3PO get lost?
He went on an R2-DTOUR.

I have four eyes, two mouths and five ears, what am I?
Ugly.

Why do golfers wear two pairs of socks?
In case they get a hole in one.

What do you call a baby turkey?
A goblet.

What did the femur say to the patella?
"Let's blow this joint."

Which of the burger say to the bun?
"Let us get together and catch up."

What is it called when a cat wins the dog show?
Cat-has-trophy.

Did you hear about the shampoo shortage in Jamaica?
It's dreadful.

What do you do when there's a sink standing outside your door?
You let that sink in.

What's the difference between a crocodile and alligator?
One will see you in a while and the other will see you later.

Why can't do animals take tests?
There are too many cheetahs.

What did one bean say to the other bean?
How you bean?

What do bulls do when they go shopping?
They charge.

We're do boats go when they get sick?
The dock.

What did one plate say to the other?
Dinner is on me.

What kind of flower doesn't sleep at night?
The day-zzz.

Why shouldn't you become a vegetarian?
It's a huge missed steak.

Did you hear I put all my spare cash into an origami business?
It folded.

Did you hear about the guy who made a car out of spaghetti?
He saw his mom and went pasta.

What does C.S. Lewis Keep at the back of his wardrobe?
Narnia business!

Why do writers constantly feel cold?
Because they're surrounded by drafts.

What does Charles Dickens keep in a spice rack?
The best of thymes the worst of thymes.

What did one boat say to the other? **Are you up for a little row-mance?**

Which is faster heat or cold?
Heat because you can catch cold!

What do you call a really big psychic?
A four chin teller.

Where do crayons go on vacation?
Colorado.

Why did the belt get arrested?
He held up a pair of pants.

Would you lawyers wear to court?
Lawsuits.

What do you call a cow with a twitch?
Beef jerky.

Did you hear about the joke about the roof?
Never mind it's over your head.

What three candies can you find in every school?
Nerds, Dum Dums and Smarties.

What do you call a bee that lives in America?
USB.

What did the fishermen say the magician?
Pick a cod, any cod!

Why did the can crusher quit his job?
Because it was soda pressing.

Why couldn't the sesame seed leave the casino?
Because he was on a roll.

Why did the yogurt go to the art exhibit?
Because it was cultured.

What's the difference between an African elephant and an Indian elephant?
About five thousand miles!

What did the daddy tomato say to the baby tomato?
Catch up!

What's the best damn program on TV?
A documentary about beavers.

Where does Batman go to do his business?
The Batroom.

Why don't steak jokes work?
They are never well done.

What do you call a frog with no legs?
Unhoppy.

What the funniest candy bar?
Snickers.

Will you call a bear with no socks on?
Barefoot.

Why did Tony go out with the prune?
Because he couldn't find a date.

Did you hear about the guy who got hit in the head with a can of soda?
It's ok; it was just a soft drink.

What do the little mountain say to the big mountain?
"Hi, Cliff."

What washes up on very small beaches?
Microwaves.

What happened when the skunk walked
into the courtroom?
There was odor and the court.

Will you call Mom and Dad ghosts?
Transparents.

Why did the tomato turn red?
It saw the salad dressing.

What street do ghost haunt?
Dead ends.

What's a skeleton's favorite form of art?
Skull-ptures.

Why don't blind people eat fish?
Because they can't see food.

What did the Canadian eagle say?
"I am soar-y."

What's the smelliest hair?
Nose hair.

What did the girl quit her job at the doughnut factory?
She was fed up with the hole business.

How do you learn to drive stick shift?
Find a manual.

How did the hipster eat his hot dog?
With a man bun.

How did the long distance relationship go?
So far, so good.

Why shouldn't you like giraffes?
They are in-tall-erable.

What did baby corn ask mama corn?
"Where is pop corn?"

What did the grape do when he got
stepped on?
He let out a little wine.

Did you hear about the joke about the
German sausage?
It was the wurst.

Did you hear about the cheese factory
explosion in France?
There was nothing left but de brie.

What do you call a man with a rubber
toe?
Roberto.

What do you get when you cross a
snowman with a Vampire?
Frostbite.

What do you call a fish with two knees?
A two knee fish.

What's the loudest pet you can buy?
A trumpet.

Why did the vampire attack Taylor Swift?
She had bad blood.

What should you do if you keep burning your Hawaiian pizzas?
Put it on Aloha setting.

What would happen if I saw a big cat escape his cage?
I'd puma my pants.

How do you count cows?
With a cow-culator.

What's the marsupial's favorite cocktail?
A pina koala.

What did the blanket say to the bed?
Don't worry I got you covered!

Which U.S. state has the smallest soft drinks?
Mini-soda.

What did the duck say to the bartender?
"Put it on my bill."

What kind of tea is hard to swallow?
Reality.

What kind of lights did Noah have on the ark?
Floodlights.

You have a bookmark?
Yes, but my name is Brian.

Why do goldfish like to hide in ponds?
They are just being koi.

Why did the blind man fall down the well?
He just didn't see that well.

Why couldn't lifeguard see the hippie?
He was too far out, man.

What did the man say before he kicked the bucket?
"How far do you think I can kick this bucket?"

How do you find Will Smith in the snow?
Look for fresh prints.

How much do human bones weigh?
A skele-ton.

What time did the man go to the dentist?
Tooth hurty.

What happened when 1 and 20 played a game together?
21.

Why did the police officer arrest the chicken?
He suspected fowl play.

How do you stop eating at Thanksgiving?
Quit cold turkey.

Why can't Pirates finish the alphabet?
Because we get lost at 'C'!

What do you call a monster with no neck?
The lost neck monster.

How did the dentist become a brain surgeon?
His hand slipped.

Why do shoemakers go to heaven?
Because they have good souls.

How does NASA organize a party?
They planet.

Why are koalas actually bears?
They don't meet the koalafications.

What do you get when you cross a dyslexic an insomniac and an agnostic?
Someone who lies awake at night wondering if there's a dog.

What do you call a bear with no ears?
B!

What stores have the most problems?
Magazine stores, they always have issues!

Why do birds fly south for the winter?
Because it's too far to walk.

Why was the broom late?
It overslept.

How do you know if you have a heavy
red-hot chili pepper?
**Give it a weigh, give it a weigh, give it
a weigh now...**

What happens if you eat yeast and shoe
polish?
Every morning you'll rise and shine!

What did the doctor say to the man about
his bladder infection?
Urine trouble!

What do you call an alligator in a vest?
An investigator.

How does a woman know her wedding
was beautiful?
Even the cake will be in tiers.

What did Jay-Z call his girlfriend before they were married?
Feyonce.

Why do vampires believe everything you tell him?
Because they're suckers.

Does anyone need an ark?
Because I Noah guy!

What's red and bad for your teeth?
A brick.

What did the hamburger name is daughter?
Patty.

Will you call a teacher never passes gas in public?
A private tutor.

What kind of egg do bad chickens like?
A deviled egg.

How do you repair a broken tomato?
Tomato paste.

Why are dogs bad dancers?
Because they have two left feet!

Why do they tell actors to break a leg?
Because every play has a cast.

Why are frogs so happy?
They eat whatever bugs them.

Why are there no zippers on pants in Syria?
It's a no-fly zone.

How did people apologize back in the day?
Remorse code.

What did the janitor say when he jumped out the closet?
"Supplies!"

Why is there a fence around cemeteries?
Because people are just dying to get in.

What did the vegetable say to at the party?
"Lettuce turnip the beet!"

With a pirate's favorite letter?
You think it's R but it's the C.

What did the green grape say the purple grape?
"Breathe, breathe!"

Have you heard about corduroy pillows?
They're making headlines.

What do Alexander the Great and Kermit the Frog have in common?
Same middle name.

Do Australian's take cream?
No they just have coffee, mate.

Why was the king one foot tall?
Because he was a ruler.

What do you call two carnivores fighting?
A beef.

What did the woman say when she saw her gray hair?
"I feel like dyeing."

How did Darth Vader know what Luke for Christmas?
He felt his presents.

What did one wall say to the other?
Meet you at the corner.

What do you call a belt made out of watches?
A waist of time.

What do you call a computer that sings?
Adele.

Why did the man lose his job at the orange juice factory?
He couldn't concentrate.

What do you call a South American girl who's always in a hurry?
Urgent Tina.

How did the farmer mend his pants?
With cabbage patches.

What do the tailor think of his new job?
It was sew sew.

Why can't the pirate play cards?
Because he was sitting on the deck.

What did one elevator say to the other elevator?
I think I'm coming down with something.

Did you hear the one about the geologist?
He took his wife for granite.

What did the insulation say to the house?
"No guarantees but I'll do asbestos I can!"

What do you call a blind deer?
No eye-deer.

What is Forrest Gump's password?
1forrest1.

What kind of classical music do chickens like?
Bach Bach Bach!

Did you hear about the ghost comedian?
He was boo-ed off stage.

What do you get if you cross a car game with typhoon?
Bridge Over Troubled Water.

How do spiders communicate?
The worldwide web.

Did you hear about the limo driver who went 25 years without a customer?
All that time and nothing to chauffer it.

How do you turn a duck into a soul singer?
Put in the microwave until it's Bill Withers.

What did the cannibal say when he ate the clown?
"Does this taste funny to you?"

Why should you respect clones?
Because they're people two.

What did Adam say before the day before Christmas?
It's Christmas, Eve.

Why do seagulls fly over the sea?
Because if they flew over the bay they'd be bay-gulls.

What do you call an 80s pop band with a scoop of ice cream?
Depeche a la mode.

What do you call a group of men waiting for a haircut?
A barber que.

What do you call a frozen dog?
A pupsicle.

How do you keep a bagel from getting away?
Put lox on it.

Why can't a woman ask her brother for help?
Because he can't be a brother and a sister too.

Why were all the ink spots crying?
Their father was in a pen.

Why can't you explain puns to kleptomaniacs?
They always take things literally.

What do you call a dog that can do magic?
Labracadabrador.

Why couldn't the bike stand up by itself?
It was two tired.

How many tickles does it take to make an octopus laugh?
Ten tickles.

What do prisoners use to call each other?
Cell phones.

Why did the Cyclops close his school?
Because he only had one people.

Why did the man sell his vacuum?
It didn't do anything but collect dust.

What do sprinters eat before a race?
Nothing, they just fast.

How do snails fight?
They slug it out.

Why was the Mexican food cold?
Because it was a little brrrrrrito.

How do you know when you're drowning
in milk?
When it's past your eyes.

How often can you tell jokes about
chemistry?
Periodically.

Why were all the dogwood trees silent?
They lost their bark.

What do you call a person who tells dad
jokes but has no kids?
A faux pa.

Why can't two elephants go swimming?
**Because they only have one pair of
trunks.**

What rhymes with orange?
No it doesn't.

Why do chicken coops only have two doors?
Because if they had four doors it be a chicken sedan.

What do French people eat snails?
Because they don't like fast food.

Why are dogs bad storytellers?
Because they only have one tail.

How much room should you give a fungi to grow?
As mushroom as possible.

How does trees get online?
It just logs in.

What happened to the man who tried to sue the airport for misplacing his luggage?
He lost his case.

Did you hear about the man who was accidentally buried alive?
It was a grave mistake.

What happened to the man who ran behind the car?
He was exhausted.

What happened to the man who ran in front of the car?
He was tired.

Have you heard about the new restaurant called karma?
There's no menu, you get what you deserve.

What's the worst part about getting electrocuted?
It Hertz.

Why did the man name his phone Titanic?
He wanted to see the Titanic synching.

Why did Christopher Columbus hate poker?
He could never beat the straits of Magellan.

What did the termite say when he walked into the bar?
"Is the bar tender here?"

What do you call a cow that just gave birth?
De-calf-einated.

If you're going out to dinner how should you look?
With your eyes.

Are you alright?
No I'm half left.

What do you call a hen looking at our lettuce?
Chicken sees our salad.

Why happened when the man became a professional leaf collector?
He started raking it in.

What do you get if you stand between two llamas?
Llama-nated.

Why did the man love the rotation of the earth?
Because it really made his day.

Where does The Lone Ranger take his trash?
To the dump to the dump to the dump dump dump to the dump to the dump to the dump dump dump...

Would you call a funny man from Africa?
Malarious.

What does the cat say when its mouth hurts?
Meow-uth!

What's a palindrome?
No it isn't.

What do you call something that doesn't have a mass?
Not Catholic.

Why should the number 288 never be mentioned?
It's too gross.

What did Al Gore playing on his guitar?
An algorithm.

Why do mathematicians like parks?
Because of all the natural logs.

Did you hear about the net new broom?
It's sweeping the nation.

What did Mississippi by Virginia?
A New Jersey.

What did Delaware?
I don't know, Alaska.

What do you get from a pampered cow?
Spoiled milk.

Man walks into a library and says, "Can I have a cheeseburger? The librarian says, "Sir this is a library!" The man whispers, "I'm sorry, can I have a cheeseburger?"

What ends with an E and has lots of letters in it?
The Post Office.

What kind of news does the ocean follow?
Current.

Which cat is the most delicious?
Kit Kat.

What do you call storm troopers playing Monopoly?
A game of Clones.

What do you call a lamb covered in chocolate?
A candy baaaaaa.

What's a keyboard's blood type?
Typ-o!

A bear walks into a restaurant. The waiter asks him what he would like. The bear says, "A steak … and a salad." The waiter says, "Why the big paws?"

How many squirrels does it take to change a light bulb?

Actually, none because squirrels only change bulbs that are nut broken.

Which famous person do you get when you make a wreath out of $100 bills?

Aretha Franklin!

Why did the insomniac man get arrested?

He resisted a rest.

Why did the king go to the dentist?

To get his teeth crowned!

What did the painter say to her boyfriend?

"I love you with all my art!"

When does a joke become a dad joke?

When the punch line become apparent.

THE END

Made in the USA
Middletown, DE
16 December 2019